9/12

Bruno Mars

ABDO
Publishing Company

Big Buddy BOOKS
Buddy Bios

by **Sarah Tieck**

VISIT US AT
www.abdopublishing.com

Published by ABDO Publishing Company, PO Box 398166, Minneapolis, MN 55439.

Printed in the United States of America, North Mankato, Minnesota.
102011
012012
 PRINTED ON RECYCLED PAPER

Coordinating Series Editor: Rochelle Baltzer
Contributing Editors: Megan M. Gunderson, BreAnn Rumsch, Marcia Zappa
Graphic Design: Maria Hosley
Cover Photograph: *AP Photo*: Peter Kramer.
Interior Photographs/Illustrations: *AP Photo*: Paul Abell/PictureGroup via AP IMAGES (p. 17), AP Photo (p. 8), The Canadian Press, Darren Calabrese (p. 29), Jeff Christensen, file (p. 12), Jeff Daly/PictureGroup via AP IMAGES (p. 7), Mark Davis/PictureGroup via AP IMAGES (p. 17), Gregg DeGuire/PictureGroup via AP IMAGES (p. 15), Kristian Dowling/PictureGroup via AP IMAGES (p. 18), Richard Drew (p. 25), Scott Gries/PictureGroup via AP IMAGES (p. 5), Peter Kramer (pp. 17, 19), Matt Sayles (p. 23), Ian West/PA Wire URN:10045092 Press Association via AP Images (p. 23); *Getty Images*: Andy Kropa (p. 27), Catherine McGann (p. 9), Frank Micelotta/ImageDirect (p. 10), Nick Pickles (p. 21), Kevin Winter (p. 11).

Library of Congress Cataloging-in-Publication Data

Tieck, Sarah, 1976-
  Bruno Mars : popular singer & songwriter / Sarah Tieck.
    p. cm. -- (Big buddy biographies)
  ISBN 978-1-61783-226-0
  1. Mars, Bruno--Juvenile literature. 2. Musicians--United States--Biography--Juvenile literature. I. Title.
  ML3930.M318T54 2012
  782.42164092--dc23
  [B]
                        2011040761

Bruno Mars

Contents

Bruno comes from a family of performers. So, he isn't shy about meeting fans or getting onstage.

Rising Star

Bruno Mars is a talented singer and songwriter. He is best known for singing and writing popular music. Fans around the world love his songs!

Hawaii

Honolulu

N
W E
S

PACIFIC
OCEAN

Family Ties

Bruno Mars's real name is Peter Gene Hernandez. He was born in Honolulu, Hawaii, on October 8, 1985.

Bruno has a large family. His parents are Bernadette "Bernie" and Pete Hernandez. Bruno's brother is named Eric. His sisters are Jaime, Tiara, Tahiti, and Presley.

Bruno's family is very proud of his success. They enjoy seeing him onstage.

Did you know...

Bruno's family chose his nickname because he reminded them of famous wrestler Bruno Sammartino. He changed his last name to Mars years later when fans said he was "out of this world."

Little Elvis

Bruno's parents were musicians. They shared their love of music with their children. They listened to **reggae**, rock, **hip-hop**, and **rhythm and blues** music. When Bruno was just four years old, he began **performing** in shows with his family. He **impersonated** famous singer Elvis Presley. Bruno became known as Little Elvis. People were surprised by how much he acted like the real Elvis!

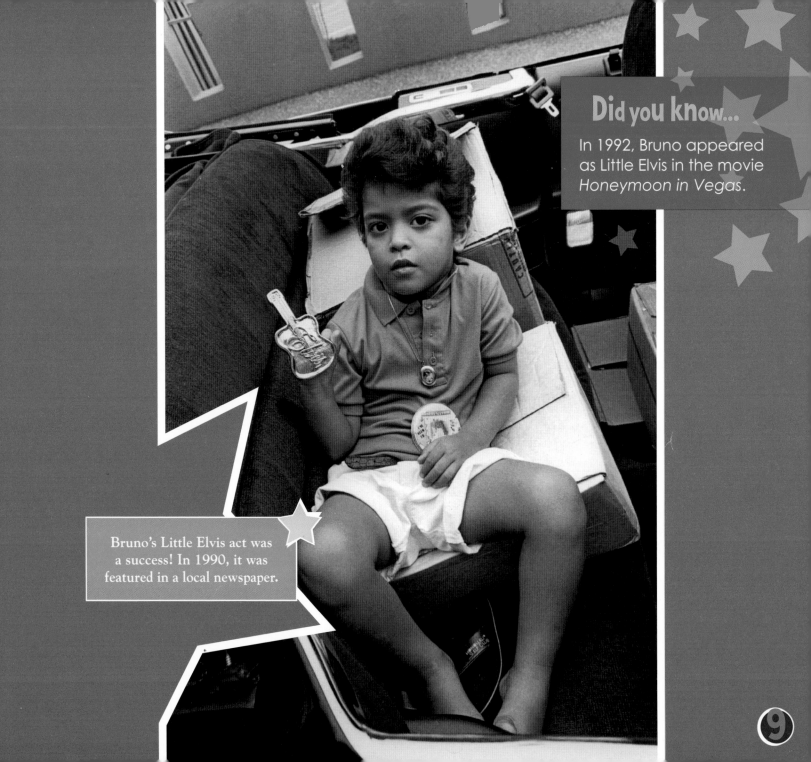

9

Michael Jackson (*center*) was known as the King of Pop.

As Bruno grew older, he began **impersonating** famous singer Michael Jackson. People loved Bruno's work!

In high school, Bruno and some friends formed a band called the School Boys. They sang 1950s, 1960s, and 1970s songs called oldies. They **performed** in hotels in Honolulu.

Did you know...
Bruno attended Roosevelt High School in Honolulu.

Bruno gets some of his music and dancing ideas from famous artists of the past.

Bruno is known for his big hairstyles. He is also known for wearing hats, such as fedoras.

Becoming an Artist

Bruno was a good **performer** and he enjoyed **impersonating** other singers. But, he wanted to make his own music and choose his own style.

So after high school, Bruno moved to Los Angeles, California. He hoped to become a music artist. At first, he had to get a regular job to pay his bills.

Bruno didn't forget his dream. He worked hard writing songs, and he sent them to record companies. But, music **executives** wanted other people to sing Bruno's songs. Bruno was let down. Then, he saw this as a way to get started in the music business.

So, Bruno kept writing songs. He also worked as a **producer**. During this time, he got to know himself better. He wrote about his life and feelings using his favorite music styles, such as **hip-hop**.

15

Making Music

As a songwriter and **producer**, Bruno has worked with many well-known artists. He helped write Flo Rida's "Right Round." In February 2009, this song was a number one hit!

Bruno also worked with Matisyahu to write "One Day." This song was used during the 2010 Winter Olympics.

Bruno has helped write songs for artists including Flo Rida (*left*), K'Naan (*right*), and Cee Lo Green (*below*).

A Star Is Born

Bruno kept busy writing and **producing** songs for other singers. But, he still wanted to become a singer himself. After he wrote a song, he would sing the **demo**. Soon, people noticed Bruno's singing talent!

In spring 2010, Bruno helped write "Nothin' On You" for **rapper** B.o.B. That summer, he helped write Travie McCoy's "Billionaire." Bruno had singing parts for each song! Both songs became very popular.

When Bruno works with other artists, such as B.o.B. (*right*) and Travie McCoy (*below right*), it is called collaborating.

First Album

Finally, Bruno had the chance to record his own album! In summer 2010, he released "Just the Way You Are" before his album came out. The song was a hit!

That fall, Bruno released *Doo-Wops & Hooligans*. Hit songs on the album include "Grenade" and "The Lazy Song."

DOO-WOPS & HOOLIGANS

Bruno's favorite music styles can be heard on his first album.

A Musical Life

Bruno spends many hours writing and recording music. He also practices singing and dancing before **performing**. Performing live onstage is one of Bruno's favorite things. He says his music is best experienced live.

Bruno has appeared in magazines. And, he has been a guest on television and radio shows (*below*).

Bruno is a skilled dancer. He shows off his talent in videos and onstage.

Bruno also goes on concert tours to help his music become known. When he is on tour, Bruno may spend months away from home. He travels to cities around the world and **performs** live concerts.

Bruno also attends events and meets fans. His fans are always excited to see him!

Reporters often take Bruno's picture.
And, fans ask for his autograph.

25

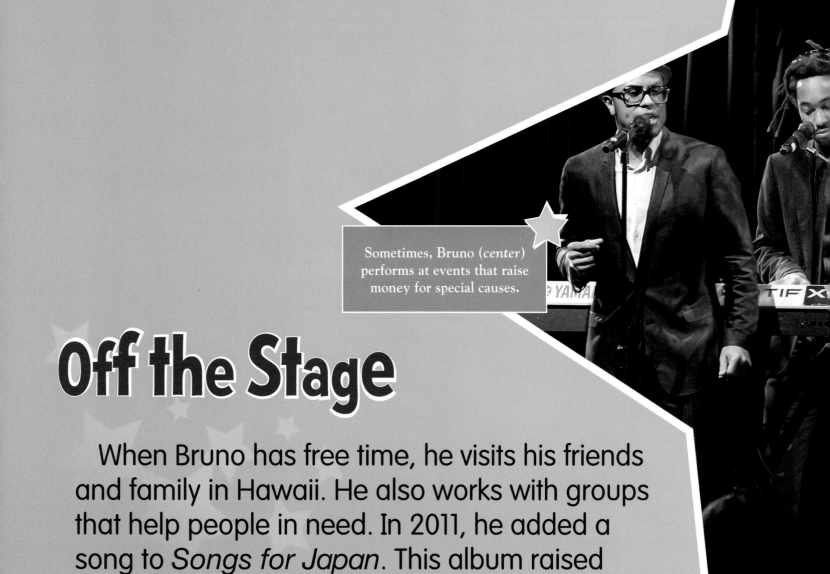

Sometimes, Bruno (*center*) performs at events that raise money for special causes.

Off the Stage

When Bruno has free time, he visits his friends and family in Hawaii. He also works with groups that help people in need. In 2011, he added a song to *Songs for Japan*. This album raised money after a major tsunami. Also in 2011, Bruno helped raise money to feed children in Africa.

Many people have noticed Bruno's fashion style. Some say he looks like famous stars from the past.

Buzz

Bruno's opportunities continue to grow. In 2011, he wrote and sang "It Will Rain." This song was in the movie *The Twilight Saga: Breaking Dawn - Part 1*. Fans are excited to see what Bruno will sing and write next!

Snapshot

★**Name**: Peter Gene "Bruno Mars" Hernandez

★**Birthday**: October 8, 1985

★**Birthplace**: Honolulu, Hawaii

★**Album**: *Doo-Wops & Hooligans*

Important Words

demo a recording to show a musical group or artist's abilities.

executive (ihg-ZEH-kyuh-tihv) a high-level employee who manages or directs a company.

hip-hop a form of popular music that features rhyme, spoken words, and electronic sounds. It is similar to rap music.

impersonate (ihm-PUHR-suh-nayt) to copy the actions of or pretend to be another person.

perform to do something in front of an audience.

producer a person who oversees the making of a movie, a play, an album, or a radio or television show.

rapper someone who raps. To rap is to speak the words of a song to a beat.

reggae (REH-gay) a form of popular music that has a strong beat. It began in Jamaica in the 1960s.

release to make available to the public.

rhythm (RIH-thuhm) **and blues** a form of popular music that features a strong beat. It is inspired by jazz, gospel, and blues styles.

Web Sites

To learn more about Bruno Mars, visit ABDO Publishing Company online. Web sites about Bruno Mars are featured on our Book Links page. These links are routinely monitored and updated to provide the most current information available.

www.abdopublishing.com

Index